Home, Sweet TOXIC Home

97 Ways Your House Can Make You Sick

Barry Jones

 CONSUMER'S CHOICE PUBLISHING

This book is intended for anyone interested in living in a more healthful indoor environment as a simple, easy to read, issue by issue, room by room guide and checklist to identify and avoid potentially harmful exposures in their homes.

The author claims no scientific or medical credentials but is an individual who developed environmental illness and has done over sixteen years of research on related topics in the process of rebuilding his health. His purpose in writing this book is not to discuss the specific chemistry of household pollutants. A number of books have been written for that purpose and several are recommended herein.

The content of this book is not medical advice nor is it intended to replace medical care. Always consult your physician before changing any medications or treatments.

It is not always possible to determine a single cause for health problems. In many cases environmental exposures are only part of the cause.

The publisher and the author are not responsible for any goods and/or services offered or referred to in this book and expressly disclaim all liability in connection with the fulfillment of orders for any such goods and/or services and for any damage, loss, or expense to person or property arising out of or relating to them.

The identities of people described in the case stories have been changed to protect client confidentiality. The author thanks every one of these people for being a part of his life and this book!

Author: Barry Jones
Editor: Michele Jones
Cover Design: Charlotte Krebs / Salmagundi Design Studio
Layout Design: Michele Jones

Home, Sweet, TOXIC Home is available in quantity from CONSUMER'S CHOICE PUBLISHING, P.O. Box 31718, Tucson, Arizona, USA 85751 or email info@yourhealthyhome.com.

Printed in the United States of America.

ACKNOWLEDGMENTS

While many people have a lifelong desire to write a book, I must confess I wasn't one of them. I was, however, very fortunate to have the encouragement and support of family members, friends and clients who believed in me and this project.

First and foremost, I will be forever grateful to my loving wife, Michele, for her encouragement, research, editing and layout/design work. Without her help this book wouldn't exist.

I am also truly blessed to have a group of wonderful friends who have proofread and/or offered their valuable input throughout the process. I'd like to sincerely thank: Don and Adele, Gayle and Ellwyn, Bob, Eric and Missy, Bill and Wilma, Michael, John and Jennifer, Mitchell, Justin, Frank and Mary Ann and Jack.

And finally, my sincere thanks to all of my clients who have allowed me to share their stories with you.

CONTENTS

FOREWORD

In 1962, Dr. Theron Randolph attended a conference on air pollution in Washington, D.C. At that conference Dr. Randolph expressed concern that no mention had been made of <u>indoor</u> air pollution. *He said he found indoor air pollution to be eight to ten times more important as a cause of chronic illness in susceptible / sensitive people than outdoor air pollution.*

- Over 3 decades later a recently completed twelve year study reports a *73%* increase in the number of children diagnosed with asthma each year.

- Last year asthma alone was responsible for 1.8 million emergency room visits, 5,000 deaths and more than 10 million missed days of school.

- The *Centers for Disease Control* (CDC) estimated asthma related costs at $6.2 billion in 1999 and projected a substantial increase for 2000. Many experts believe indoor air pollution is a major factor.

- Some are referring to this shocking increase in the number of asthma cases as *"<u>the asthma epidemic</u>."*

- A recent magazine article on building-related illness predicted the percentage of the population (5-10%) that is allergic / reactive to chemicals <u>will increase to 60%</u> by 2020.

It is small wonder that prescription and over-the-counter medications for respiratory problems are among the fastest growing categories of pharmaceuticals. A friend of ours who owned a chain of pharmacies tells us when he started that business they ordered inhalers a case of six at a time and sometimes their expiration dates caused them to be disposed of before they could be sold. By contrast, today those same pharmacies regularly order many cases per week.

We're aware of the tragedy of Fetal Alcohol Syndrome and the effects of smoking during pregnancy. It is now estimated that 60% or more of the population is suffering negative health effects due to ongoing exposure to polluted indoor environments. Is it too great a stretch to suspect that regular inhalation of other environmental pollutants during pregnancy may contribute to a baby's future health problems? Homes, schools, offices, virtually all occupied buildings contain pollutants that negatively impact their occupants' health.

Many chronically ill people are being tested, treated and/or counseled for health problems that can't quite be explained or even identified. Headaches, fatigue, shortness of breath, depression, ADHD, difficulty concentrating, heart rhythm irregularities, digestive problems, sleep disturbances, ringing ears, muscle aches ... *and the list goes on*. To many medical practitioners this laundry list of symptoms sounds like hypochondria. Unfortunately, many doctors don't yet consider environmental exposures as a cause of illness when treating their patients.

The GOOD News!

Fortunately, a little knowledge and a few common sense changes can make a big difference, not only for those who are already sick but also for those who will become sick if they do not become more environmentally aware. The information in this book is essential for anyone who wants to take the next important step in creating a healthier and safer lifestyle by living in a *Healthy Home Environment*.

Parents with small children should pay particular attention to these issues because lifelong health patterns are established during a child's formative years, when they are most vulnerable to environmental pollutants.

Individuals recovering from any illness or surgery are also more susceptible to indoor pollutants and a healthy environment plays an important role in their recovery.

INTRODUCTION

Chronic illness is <u>not</u> the natural human condition. Most of us are born with the gift of health. Then many of us become chronically ill through poor diet, lack of exercise, emotional stress and *yes*, environmental influences. Some of us suffer "ignorable symptoms," such as congestion, occasional headaches, lethargy, muscle stiffness, joint pain, indigestion, lack of mental clarity, etc., etc. Often, we accept these symptoms as a fact of life, telling ourselves *"I'm getting older"* or *"Everyone I know is the same."* The fact is, many of these difficulties are the result of things we have done or <u>not</u> done to and for ourselves. Sometimes, as in my case, the symptoms were *not* ignorable and were in fact a serious illness caused by controllable pollutants in my home environment.

The cause of my symptoms, and the focus of this book, is environmentally caused illness. *Imagine* –simply buying a common household cleaning product, bringing it home and inadvertently leaving the container open in your home could <u>DESTROY</u> your health! It certainly can and it's happening every day. My purpose in writing this book is to call attention to these issues and alert you to the importance of living in a healthy home.

The recommendations in this book are based on exhaustive personal research and experience, coupled with plain old common sense. I'm not a doctor or a scientist and have no scientific credentials. I'm not even a writer. I'm a person who became seriously ill and could find no help within the medical system. As you will read in Chapter 1, I searched diligently and found none. Over the last 16 years I have done extensive research on these issues and worked with hundreds of people who were living in seriously unhealthy homes. Some of these homes were immaculately maintained and worth well over a million dollars. So, if you think these issues affect only part of the socio-economic spectrum, think again! <u>Every</u> neighborhood has families whose health is being negatively impacted.

Some experts say we live in too clean an environment, claiming that our immunity is underdeveloped because we lack regular exposure to organic pollutants, like animal waste, that once surrounded our ancestors in their rural environments, thereby helping them to develop natural immunities. While I believe there is something to that theory, please bear in mind that many of these experts are researchers who receive grant money for research focused on the <u>application</u>, not *avoidance* of chemicals and drugs. Their perspective is understandably pro-chemical. By contrast, I am personally convinced we need fewer chemicals, not more cow manure, in our living environment.

If you're a scientist looking for cause and effect documentation in this book, you'll be disappointed. I didn't write this book for the scientific community. ***Too many people are sick!*** We can't wait for scientifically verifiable evidence that a certain concentration of a specific chemical gas in a typical home will have a given adverse effect on a minimum percentage of a group of people in a double blind study. Where environmentally caused illness is concerned, there are too many variables and too many differences in individual susceptibility to prove cause and effect in most cases. It is the <u>long-term daily exposure to low levels of *numerous* pollutants</u> that causes the greatest harm, eroding our health one breath at a time. Concentrations of particles, chemical gasses and biological contaminants are constantly changing and can be sufficiently potent to make one family member seriously ill for months or even years before the rest of the family is noticeably affected.

Home Environment Center

After years of searching for and experimenting with various products to create a healthy living environment, my wife and I opened the *Home Environment Center* in Tucson, Arizona. We personally use and represent many of the products recommended in this book and are seeking and testing new products on a regular basis.

Over the past 16 years I have shared my story and the information you are about to read to educate and help people who are experiencing difficulties or severe illness that may well be related to or caused by their indoor environments. I sincerely thank you for taking the time to become more aware of this issue and encourage you to share this book with those you love.

Barry Jones, *Tucson, Arizona*

– 1 –
A Life Changing Event

The morning sun warmed my back as I walked across the parking lot to my office — one of those beautiful, late September mornings when the texture and smell of the air signals the end of another hot (but dry) Arizona summer. The birds were singing as children walked by on their way to school. I had been to the health club for an early workout and felt on top of the world. I am especially appreciative of days like this. Such mornings are particularly symbolic for me since it was a similar September morning sixteen years ago when my life took a dramatic, unexpected turn…

The year was 1985. As I made my way through the crowded cleaning products aisle at the local grocery store, I had no idea my life was about to change forever. I had just purchased a townhouse to establish a new residence following my divorce. To set up housekeeping I needed all sorts of products to equip my new home and was loading my cart with soaps, sponges, a mop, paper products, trash cans and bags, etc.

I was excited to begin this new phase of my life. I had a successful business, was working out regularly and was in the best shape of my life. I was also traveling extensively – Japan, the Bahamas and Mexico, all within a couple of months. My townhouse was a place I seldom spent any time, other than to sleep.

During the first few weeks in my new home I developed what I thought was a cold. I had a bit of a sore throat, sinus irritation and just didn't feel well. I finally went to see a doctor who gave me an antibiotic. Two weeks later I was no better, went back to the doctor and was prescribed another round of the antibiotic.

I then began to experience severe fatigue, digestive problems and noticed I was losing weight. As I saw other doctors for various tests, I became concerned that something was seriously wrong. We considered and tested for a number of things including parasites (possibly picked up while I was out of the country), infectious diseases, one blood test after another, yet discovered no clue why I was so sick. Every test came back negative.

By month four I had completely lost my sense of smell and still had no diagnosis. I made my way from one doctor to another hoping someone could help me. When I moved into my townhouse I weighed 195 pounds. Five months later I was down to 158. When I met with each new doctor, I carried with me a 3 x 5 card with a list of my symptoms. The list filled both sides. My memory was so bad I couldn't even recite all of the more serious symptoms for the doctors I was seeing.

Imagine my frustration as I heard one doctor after another ask me which ONE symptom bothered me the most. How could I choose between the inability to control my left arm and leg, the fact that I couldn't focus my mind to even construct a proper sentence, my wasting away to skin and bones or the debilitating abdominal cramping every time I ate something? Perhaps the severe fatigue, blurred vision and extreme sensitivity to chemicals would have been better choices. What would your selection have been?

As my condition worsened and my concern and frustration grew, I started changing doctors more quickly, believing I just hadn't yet found the doctor who could identify the cause of my illness. All this time, by the way, not even one of the medical practitioners I saw asked about my home, the air I was breathing or the water I was drinking. I saw MD's, chiropractors, naturopaths and osteopaths, one after another. I was feeling like a square peg and all they had were round holes. There just didn't seem to be an answer to why I was so sick.

If I had been 90 years old I could have understood why I felt so awful. If my body was simply worn out and I was nearing the end of my life, I could have accepted my condition. But I wasn't 90, I was only 35! And at age 35 I had reached a point where I was concerned I was going to die and never know the reason why. Then the inevitable happened. A doctor decided my problem was psychological. He said I needed to see a psychologist. I certainly didn't expect that! After a moment's thought, I said, "If you really believe that's my problem, pick one and I'll go. I just want to identify my problem and get to work on getting better."

I now believe many people suffer from depression and other psychological problems caused by environmental illness. The most troubling cases are the children being fed prescription narcotics to make them behave when their problem may be the mold and chemicals, etc. in their schools and homes (more about that later).

Imagine my good fortune! The shrink said he was confident my problem was physical and I should continue my search. But wait! When the doctor got the report ... YOU GUESSED IT! He said I'd better see a *different* shrink! Fortunately, the second shrink came to the same conclusion as the first, and two shrinks was my limit. I wasn't going to be "shopped around" until someone decided to medicate me to the point where I wouldn't care how sick I was.

My condition was still worsening and now I had a rash nearly head to toe. When I asked the next doctor why I had this rash, having never had a rash in my life, he said, "You've never been 35 years old before." Please don't EVER accept an answer like that! Something other than your birthday has caused your problem. If a doctor doesn't have a better answer than that, find another doctor.

At this point eleven months had passed and I had spent nearly ten thousand dollars on doctors since first realizing I was sick. I had accumulated an extensive library of books on every sort of health-related topic. In my desperation I was spending several hours each week at our local university medical center library looking for some clue to my illness. I alternated between anger and frustration, hopelessness and resignation. Every time I found a new possibility to pursue I became hopeful, then disappointed. Who would have guessed my breakthrough would be accidental?

Home, Sweet, TOXIC Home

I had not been out of town for several months and decided to go see a doctor in Las Vegas that a dentist friend recommended. I was gone for three days and was feeling a little stronger when I returned home. I went to bed early that night and woke up the next morning feeling like I'd been run over by a bus. *I immediately thought (for the first time) that something in my house must be making me sick. It was a gut-level, instinctual feeling.* I first suspected carbon monoxide and had the gas company come out and test the furnace. No problem. Then I called the pest control people and quizzed them. No apparent problem there either.

Next, I called the University Medical Center and was referred to two experts, Ph.D.'s who came out and collected air samples for testing and found "nothing." I later learned that among other things they didn't test for chlorine. Since I was still convinced that <u>something</u> in that townhouse was making me sick, I decided then and there to sell my home. I packed my clothes and moved out. I called a realtor and listed the house for sale. During the five months it took to sell, my sense of smell returned and some of my other symptoms were improving.

When the buyer's financing was approved I went in to quickly pack the rest of my things and that's when I discovered the cause of my illness. The last things I packed were the items under the sink in the master bathroom. When I opened the cabinet doors, the chlorine odor was overwhelming. I started pulling things out and discovered an open container of crystals that should have gone in the toilet tank to make the water blue. The active ingredient was a chlorine derivative. *I had been breathing low levels of chlorine gas every night while I slept!* A common household cleaning product had destroyed my health in just a few short months. The people from MENSA aren't exactly begging me to join them because of my brilliant mind, but I'm not the dimmest bulb in the box either! I still can't believe I didn't figure this out sooner!

In the chapters that follow you'll read about a number of people — some very intelligent professionals, even experts in related fields, who have lived, in some cases for years, with toxic exposures even worse than mine. They just didn't connect their symptoms with their daily exposure to the common pollutants found in their homes.

If you believe someone in your family is experiencing health problems caused by your home, the following questions may help you discover the cause. Any one of these things can cause problems yet I often find all of them in the same home.

- ♦ Have you done any painting, carpeting or remodeling?

- ♦ Do you use any scented products in the house, i.e. air fresheners, potpourri, candles, incense, sprays or fabric softeners?

- Have you had any roof or plumbing leaks in the house? If yes, check the affected area(s) for mold.

- Have you changed any cleaning products recently? – including laundry products, furniture polish, laundry products, soaps or shampoos?

- Do you have any gas-fired appliances? If so, do you have a carbon monoxide detector and have you checked for gas leaks?

- Have your air ducts been inspected and/or cleaned?

- Have you had your drinking water tested lately? If not, a bacteria test would be a good idea, especially if you're on a private well.

- Do you have any new pets or pet care products in your home?

- Do you have any pest infestation problems? – Bats, bees, birds, insects, rodents, etc.?

- Do you have any pest control chemicals, including moth balls, in the house?

- Have you added any new furniture or cabinets lately?

- Do you do any arts and crafts work using paints, inks or glues in the house?

- If you live in a multi-occupancy building, are your neighbors creating or emitting pollutants and/or odors?

NOTE: In the APPENDIX you'll find the above issues in the form of a questionnaire as well as a whole house checklist to help you examine your own home after reading this book. As you read each chapter you will discover the importance of these issues.

It's All In Your Head?

Throughout my ordeal I had a number of well-meaning family members and friends who tried to convince me everything would be fine if I would simply ignore my symptoms and just live my life. Even my closest friends thought I had flipped out. I can't fault them because if the roles were reversed, I probably would have done the same. Prior to my poisoning, I thought chemically sensitive and highly allergic people were hypochondriacs and/or lunatics. Having never been sick, I couldn't conceive of such an illness and many doctors still can't! I now have a whole new respect for the effect of environmental exposures and the potential suffering they can cause.

Sixteen Years Later

The journey from environmental illness back to health is a process that takes time. In most cases recovery doesn't occur as soon as the exposure is eliminated. The first priority is limiting future exposures. *I believe the key for me was expecting a return to wellness and pursuing additional knowledge and listening to my body (not an easy thing for a man to do) — thereby connecting symptoms with exposures for the purpose of future avoidance when possible.*

I am thankful every day for the improvement in my health over the past fifteen years. Each year has been better than the one before. I have been fortunate to meet a number of medical practitioners who understand environmental illness and have been a great help to me. I have utilized diet, exercise, nutritional supplementation and have avoided as many pollutants as possible to rebuild my health. Self education is very important; fortunately, there is much more information available today and a few more doctors are willing to discuss environmental illness.

Chapter 2 will introduce you to the single most important aspect of your healthy indoor environment.

SOURCES FOR PROFESSIONAL HELP:

American Academy of Environmental Medicine
7701 East Kellogg, Suite 625
Wichita, Kansas 67207
Phone: 316-684-5500
Fax: 316-684-5709
E-mail: adminstrator@aaem.com
Web site: www.aaem.com

American Association of Naturopathic Physicians
8201 Greensboro Drive,
Suite 300
McLean, Virginia 22102
Phone: 703-610-9037
Fax: 703-610-9005
Web site: www.naturopathic.org

American Industrial Hygiene Association
2700 Prosperity Ave., Suite 250
Fairfax, VA 22031
Phone: 703-849-8888
Fax: 703-207-3561
Web site: www.aiha.org

Practical Allergy Foundation in New York (Dr. Doris Rapp)
1421 Colvin Blvd
Buffalo, New York 14223
716-875-0398
Phone: Friday Only 888-895-7277
Fax: 716-875-5399
Web site: www.drrapp.com

FOR CONSULTATIONS OR LECTURES CONTACT:

Doris Rapp Clinic
8179 E Del Cuarzo
Scottsdale, Az. 85258
Phone: 602-905-9195
Fax: 602-905-8281

American Chiropractic Association
1701 Clarendon Blvd
Arlington, VA 22209
Phone: 800-986-4636
Fax: 703-243-2593
Web site: www.amerchiro.org

– 2 –
Indoor Air Pollution

♦ The Environmental Protection Agency and the U.S. House of Representatives have identified indoor air pollution as one of our top environmental health risks.

♦ The World Health Organization (WHO) states that 40% of the buildings in the world pose a serious health risk and many experts now believe that <u>most</u> people are suffering negative health effects due to these indoor exposures.

♦ Also, according to WHO estimates, between 100 million and 150 million people worldwide suffer from asthma. The numbers have been rising steadily.

♦ For the first time in human history we are more at risk indoors than we are outdoors.

How Important is Air?

There are certain things we must have to survive, the three most important being air, water and food.

If we are deprived of food we can "survive" for months. Without water we can "survive" for a number of days. Without air the balance of our life would be measured in just a few minutes!

The typical adult human breathes over 2,000 gallons of air per day! Compare that to the 1 gallon of water we drink daily. **Doesn't it make sense that the thing we do most has the greatest effect on our health?**

But wait! There's more. Did you know that <u>inhalation</u> is second only to direct injection as the most effective method for delivering toxins into our bloodstream? The linings of our lungs absorb inhaled chemicals directly into our blood and, don't forget, <u>odors</u> **are** <u>chemicals</u>.

What Is the Most Important Air You'll Ever Breathe?

You might answer, "While I'm exercising," or "All day at work." While <u>all</u> of our air is important, the most important is the air we breathe while we <u>sleep</u>. Think about it. You lie there every night, spending approximately 1/3 of your life in bed. While you sleep, your immune system is trying to regenerate. If you are breathing the typical home's less than ideal air you are consuming valuable energy and negatively impacting your immune system. Remember, this has little to do with how good a housekeeper you are. Sometimes the "cleanest" homes are the most dangerous, so don't go getting offended, okay? *(See also Chapter 3 on Cleaning & Laundry Products.)*

One of the nation's top allergy research and treatment clinics was featured on a recent morning news program. They were reporting findings of allergy research done on young children. They said children develop allergies first to <u>indoor exposures</u>: house pets, mites, mold, etc. Outdoor allergies take longer to develop as exposures are less frequent and of shorter duration, further evidence that <u>the thing we do most has the greatest effect on us</u>.

Are we starting to get the picture?

So What <u>Is</u> This Indoor Pollution?

It's made up of three overlapping components:

Particles — Chemical Gasses — and Living Organisms

The dust **particles** in residential environments are mostly human skin and pet dander. Keep in mind the average adult sheds several pounds of skin flakes per year. Now, think about the dust in your vacuum bag. It's gray, *like dead skin*, <u>not</u> brown like the dirt outside. Let's see, how many people are there in your home? And how long have you lived there? And how many pets do you have?

Over 90% of the airborne **particles** are too small to see, too light to settle from the air and are inhaled more deeply into our lungs than are the large particles. These same small particles seldom reach a filter and are often too small to be captured even when they <u>do</u> reach a filter. And remember, even the very best filter does little or nothing to remove chemical gasses and odors in a house.

Now, here comes the "overlap." Each tiny skin particle can support and transport a number of **microbiological contaminants, such as bacteria and/or viruses.** And . . . these particles also absorb **chemical gasses** in the air. Mold spores are in the mix as well, and *not* just in humid climates. Mold problems are prevalent everywhere, even in dry climates like Arizona or Colorado.

Particles in the air, in and of themselves, are officially blamed for thousands of deaths each year. A recent EPA sponsored study, results of which were released by the *Health Effects Institute* of Cambridge, Mass., announced that a small increase in airborne particles was responsible for a 1 percent increase in the death rate and a 2-4 percent increase in hospitalization of the elderly. It stands to reason that those most susceptible, children and the elderly, are the most affected.

Particles that are widely recognized sources of respiratory difficulty in the bedroom are the **microscopic dust mites** or, more importantly, their waste and the decaying parts of the dead mites. And, as most of us know, the densest accumulation of mites is in the bed. They live in our pillows, mattresses and bed clothes and feed on our skin flakes. As a general rule, the higher the humidity, the more dust mites you have. Fortunately, dust mite proof mattress and pillow encasements will prevent the mites from freely moving into and out of your mattress and pillows.

Chemical Gasses?   *"I don't have chemical gasses in my house!"* Oh, yes, you do! Cleaning products, candles, scented products, fresh dry cleaning, furniture, pesticides, gas stoves, paint, carpet, cosmetics, cabinets, and the list goes on and on – all outgas chemicals into your indoor air.

Keep in mind that your indoor air quality is constantly changing. A pet comes in from outside, the central heat comes on, you paint your nails, you put bleach in the washing machine, etc., etc. Each of these activities adds pollutants to your air. Human respiration alone can cause unhealthy levels of carbon dioxide (CO_2) to develop in poorly ventilated rooms and even the entire house. <u>Always ventilate</u>.

In some areas radon concentrations indoors are a problem. While radon is a naturally occurring radioactive gas emanating from underground granite formations, it sometimes infiltrates homes through the slab or floor. Radon concerns are primarily linked to increased lung cancer risk with long term exposure; however, the EPA says smokers are at greater risk than nonsmokers. If you are concerned about radon exposure, see the additional information at the end of this chapter.

How Did Indoor Air Get So Polluted?

Back in the '70s we had an energy crisis and building codes were changed to conserve energy. Doors and windows were closed, cracks were sealed, heating and cooling systems were designed to keep recirculating the same air over and over. We created window glass that limits the amount of ultraviolet light entering the house and made more household products from synthetics and petroleum (plastic). We also created more potent antimicrobial cleaning products.

Our homes became capsules that sealed in all of the pollutants and sealed out the cleaning effect of fresh air. Today, nearly 3 decades later, depending on where you live, opening windows may not be a solution because the *outdoor* air is as bad or <u>worse</u> than the indoor air.

Over the past twenty-five years our indoor environments have become a <u>serious</u> problem. Just look at the reports in the news. In the '70s there were practically <u>no</u> articles on indoor air pollution, in the '80s we started to hear of Sick Building Syndrome but in the '90s we saw literally thousands of reports.

Now for the Good News!

The rest of this book is about how we solve these problems, one house at a time, starting with yours. The following chapters will help you identify and correct problems throughout your home. Case stories will illustrate the importance of these issues and may even remind you of someone you know.

It's obviously impractical to think we can completely eliminate all sources of indoor pollution. However, a heightened awareness and a few common sense changes can make a world of difference.

And please bear in mind . . . after you've done all you reasonably can to reduce the offending sources of pollution in your home, there is still a very real need for a quality air purifier. Simply by living in our homes we create sufficient pollution to negatively impact our health. A quality air purifier is a necessity if we want to live in the healthiest possible environment. Many people are discovering the benefits of breathing purified air — not to be confused with *filtered* air! **The day will come when electronic air purifiers are as common in people's homes as microwave ovens and VCR's are today.**

RECOMMENDATIONS:

- ◆ Store all cleaning products containing chlorine and petroleum distillates outside of your living area. If any ingredient ends in "-ine" or "-ene" or has three syllables or more, play it safe — Put it in the garage or storeroom. Over time many of these chemicals can degrade their containers and leak. Often, they are discovered only after someone gets sick.
- ◆ Limit the indoor use of nail polish and polish remover. Maybe it's time to go to the patio, garage or a nail salon to avoid using those chemicals in your home.
- ◆ Keep windows cracked. Sleeping in a closed room will likely expose you to unhealthy levels of carbon dioxide.
- ◆ Ventilate the garage to prevent gasses from infiltrating your living area.
- ◆ Encase your pillows and mattresses with dust mite proof covers.
- ◆ Never place a filter next to your bed. To the extent it is able to draw air to itself, it will draw particles through your breathing zone while you sleep.
- ◆ Use a vacuum cleaner with quality filtration to minimize the reintroduction of particles into the air while vacuuming. *(See Chapter 4 on Carpet & Floor Coverings.)*
- ◆ If your home has a bathroom that is seldom used, once a week run a little water in the sink, shower and tub to keep the drain trap full of water to prevent sewer gasses from entering the house.

♦ Business owners: When leasing space in a multi-occupancy building, require a paragraph in your lease preventing the landlord from leasing an adjacent space to any business creating noxious odors, fumes or gasses. Hair and nail salons, pet grooming, smoke shops, silk screening, print shops, etc. moving in next door can wreak havoc with your air quality.

RECOMMENDED PRODUCTS:

♦ *Living Air* manufactures a line of portable, *filterless*, electronic air purifiers designed to clean the air in your entire house, eliminating odors from pets, smoke, cooking, new paint and carpet, mold and mildew, while also settling particles from the air. **One unit** will produce **fresher, cleaner, healthier air** in every room of the house.

♦ *The Companion Electrostatic filter* for your air conditioning unit / furnace is washable & reusable. It's a layered fabric filter that captures particles using static attraction.

♦ *Dust mite / allergy proof pillows,* pillow covers, and mattress encasements to control mite activity.

The products listed above are all available from the
Home Environment Center.
To order, call 1-888-612-5798
or visit www.YourHealthyHome.com.

ADDITIONAL INFORMATION:

Is This Your Child Dr. Doris Rapp, MD
(ISBN 0-688-11907-7)

Surviving the Toxic Crisis Dr. William R. Kellas
(ISBN 0-963-64911-6 / ISBN 0-963-64912-4)

Consumer's Guide to Radon Reduction
EPA booklet no. 402-K92-003
(800-490-9198)

– 3 –
Cleaning and Laundry Products

WARNING!
THE MOST DANGEROUS PLACE IN YOUR HOME...

is the cabinet under the sink. Make that <u>every</u> sink!

Think about it. That's where most people keep all of their chemical cleaners, spray cans, pesticides, sponges, rags, etc., etc. It is here we often find chemicals stored together which, if combined, would create deadly gasses. Even one open or leaking container of these common chemicals could cause serious health problems.

CASE STORY: Not long ago I had a call from an acquaintance named Judy who had recently been told of my chlorine poisoning by a mutual friend. Judy had been struggling with a variety of symptoms that were as yet undiagnosed and worsening. After hearing my story, she went home and inspected the cabinets under her sinks. In the spare bathroom, within a few feet of the intake for her heating and cooling system, she found an old bleach bottle that had cracked and leaked bleach into the floor of the cabinet. It had apparently been leaking for some time because crystals had formed in much of the cabinet. This chlorine exposure may or may not have been the entire cause of her symptoms. It is safe to say, however, that chlorine gas in her house likely caused her some adverse effect.

I'm not totally opposed to the use of some chemical products but I do prefer to use non-toxic cleaners whenever possible. I suggest you ventilate the house thoroughly when any of these products are in use and never store anything indoors that contains chlorine or petroleum-based chemicals. These sorts of things belong in the garage or storeroom where there is a separation between that air space and the one you live in. There should always be adequate ventilation in these areas to prevent a buildup of potentially harmful gasses.

Choosing Household Cleaners

CASE STORY: Danny had just celebrated his 4th birthday and was once again in the emergency room for his almost weekly visit because of a severe asthma attack. Fortunately, this time Danny's mother happened to link the occurrence of Danny's attack with the weekly housecleaning. After examining her chosen cleaning products, she changed to less toxic cleaners and Danny's attacks all but disappeared.

Antimicrobial Cleaners

Dr. Doris Rapp has done extensive research on these issues and in her book, *Is This Your Child?*, she discusses the effect of antimicrobial cleaners on sensitive individuals. In some cases people suffer an almost immediate, severe reaction to these chemicals. For others, the effect is more subtle over time, but in the end can still be very detrimental. Whenever possible, I prefer to use an enzyme, colloidal or citrus-based cleaner. They usually work as well or better than the more toxic cleaners and don't cause adverse reactions for most people.

Laundry Products

Many people are sensitive to the usual variety of laundry soaps and cleaners. Some react to these chemicals when they inhale them while others react upon skin contact. Interestingly, many of the skin contact reactions result from wearing clothes that were washed with detergent in hard water because hard water causes soap and dirt to be retained in the fabric. When sensitive people wear these clothes and perspire in them the caustic nature of the soap residue irritates their skin. *(See also Chapter 7 on Water.)*

Fabric Softeners

I'm hearing from more and more people that they are reactive to bed linens and clothes that have been dried with fabric softener sheets. Once again, common sense tells us if you have difficulty breathing overnight, examine what you have contact with in your bedroom. Many times, with a little thought, you may connect your symptoms with the introduction of something new, such as a laundry product.

Skin Contact

The best way to identify a problem exposure is through systematic elimination. For instance, if you develop a skin problem it may or may not be due to an inhaled pollutant. It could be something you're coming in contact with. Think first of any new product you've recently started using. Even if you haven't changed any products, you may have developed a sensitivity to one or more of your old favorites. You may want to temporarily avoid some of these products as a test.

> *CASE STORY:* An admittedly obscure yet telling example of a skin contact related problem occurred several years ago with one of my employees. My secretary had developed little white water blisters on her hands and reported they disappeared each weekend on her days off. When a second employee developed the same problem, I was concerned! After some investigation, it turned out they were reacting to the notepaper we were using. Some leftover fliers printed on coated, glossy paper had been cut up for use as notepaper and it was the coating that caused their skin problem. We disposed of the paper and the problem was solved.

RECOMMENDATIONS:

- Inspect all of the containers under your sinks. Dispose of old or leaking containers, old rags and cleaning materials, and look for potentially hazardous products.
- Store any products containing chlorine or petroleum-based chemicals outside your living space.
- Avoid using chlorine-based products as much as possible.
- To kill bacteria in kitchen sponges, soak them outdoors in a mild solution of bleach and water.
- A useful homemade cleaner can be created by combining 3 teaspoons of Borax, 4 tablespoons of white vinegar and 2 cups of hot water.
- Pay attention to symptoms or reactions that develop while housecleaning and use alternative products to see if the problems resolve.
- Wash laundry in soft water to avoid caustic residue in fabrics.

RECOMMENDED PRODUCTS:

- *EcoH Household Cleaner* from *Alive and Wellness* is my preference for most cleaning. EcoH is a blend of colloids and wetting agents that, when combined with water, become super active separating and emulsifying dirt, grease, oil and stains. Great for cleaning everything in the house including vegetables!
- *Dust Grabber Dust Cloth* picks up dust like a magnet using electrostatic attraction. Removes allergens that may cause runny nose, watery eyes and wheezing.
- *Eureka EnviroSteamers* clean and sanitize without chemicals. Floors, upholstery, kitchen, bath, even windows come squeaky clean.

**The products listed above are all available from the
Home Environment Center.
To order, call 1-888-612-5798
or visit www.YourHealthyHome.com.**

– 4 –
Carpet and Floor Coverings

The warmth and comfort carpets provide are difficult creature comforts for many of us to give up in an effort to create a healthy home. However, you don't necessarily have to eliminate carpet to have a healthy indoor environment. A little knowledge and a few common sense changes can greatly reduce harmful exposures.

Carpet *can* be a major source of pollution indoors. It is a breeding ground for mold, bacteria and dust mites and also contains herbicides and pesticides, not to mention lead, rubber particles and chemicals from nearby industry and auto traffic. And don't forget the contributions made by pets in the house! As we walk across carpet these contaminants are disturbed and aerosolized. Remember the *Peanuts* character, "Pig Pen" with his ever-present cloud of "dust" following him? That's what you would see in a darkened, carpeted room with a bright light aimed at your feet as you walk. Some of these particles can remain in the air indefinitely for us to inhale as they float within our breathing zones. But what about toddlers? A recent study estimated that a toddler crawling around a typical carpeted house receives a daily carcinogenic exposure comparable to smoking 3 cigarettes per day! The problem is twofold: Airborne contaminants are often more concentrated near the floor and there is also the direct contact issue. Think of a baby crawling on the floor. She crawls a short distance then sits up and puts her fingers in her mouth. Everything on the carpet is now being ingested!

Now, think about the sidewalk leading to your front door. You walk through all of the outdoor pollutants that have settled from the air or been sprayed nearby and enter the house wearing shoes that carry some of that pollution into the house and into the carpet. I personally like the Japanese practice of not wearing shoes in the house or at least having shoes or slippers just for inside use. We have found getting family and friends to cooperate with this "custom" can be challenging, but well worth the effort.

Cleaning Existing Carpets

Carpet cleaning is in and of itself an enormous industry. There are many different companies and techniques, each claiming to be the best. Still, regardless of claims made, certain facts remain constant:

1) The more moisture that remains in the carpet, the more likely you are to develop a mold problem. Try to schedule carpet cleaning for drier times of the year and keep the house as open as possible for a day or two after the cleaning. I recommend you choose a low moisture method using cleaning agents that are among the least toxic and least offensive.

2) Many people are sensitive to cleaning fluids and antimicrobial agents used in carpet cleaning. If you are chemically sensitive, try to spend some time in a house that has just had its carpet cleaned by the company you want to use. It's best to get referrals from friends so you can spend some time in their homes to see if you are reactive to the cleaning solutions. Most good carpet cleaners are accustomed to dealing with these issues.

Vacuum Cleaners

The two most important issues regarding vacuums are:

1) How effective are they at collecting the debris from your carpet and...

2) How little of that debris ends up in the air while you're vacuuming

There are good uprights and good canisters. The ultimate vacuum, of course, is a central system with a good power head and high suction. One advantage of the central system is the outdoor exhaust. The outdoor air discharge makes filtration less important than with a portable upright or canister.

Portable vacuums are far more common and vary widely in features, style and price. The lightest vacuums are SELDOM the most effective and many of the HEPA equipped vacuums don't perform as well as Filtrete equipped machines due to the reduced airflow caused by the HEPA filter. Our preference for upright vacuums is the *Lindhaus HEALTHCARE proHepa* line. *Lindhaus* is one of Europe's top selling commercial vacuum manufacturers. They now offer mid-priced, high quality residential machines in the U.S. and Canada. Their balance between performance, quality, filtration, weight, features, design and price make them an <u>excellent</u> value.

If you prefer a canister, my choice is the Oxygen line of HEPA vacuums from Eureka. The Oxygen is reasonably priced and is the winner of several design awards for its style and features, including a washable HEPA filter.

Choosing New Floor Coverings

For highly allergic / sensitive people, wall to wall carpet may not be the best choice. However, if you choose a carpet and pad that passes the *Carpet and Rug Institute's* (CRI) outgassing tests, and use only a CRI approved latex adhesive to install it, you should have far less difficulty. I would also require the installer to unroll and air out the carpet and pad for a couple of days before the installation because even the best materials will outgas for a time. Wool carpets are popular with some people and, although they're generally more costly to install, they can be a wise choice for many.

Don't forget that whatever is on the slab or substrate, i.e. mold or pet urine residue, should be removed and/or neutralized before the carpet is installed. There are some very effective enzyme and colloidal cleaners available to replace toxic chemicals used for this purpose.

Floor Covering Alternatives

Tile, hardwood, vinyl, parquet – we have many choices for style and material. Once again, I would check for CRI approvals and use latex (non-petroleum) adhesives and avoid volatile sealers.

Hard floors with cotton or wool area rugs help many people maintain as allergen-free an environment as possible. The ability to dust mop the floor and throw the rugs in the washing machine provides a healthy, low maintenance option.

RECOMMENDATIONS:

♦ Use only carpets, pads and adhesives that pass the *Carpet and Rug Institute's* outgassing tests.

♦ When possible, use wood, slate, concrete, tile or linoleum flooring made from non-toxic materials. Be sure to use low or zero VOC sealers, finishes and adhesives.

♦ Use a quality, high-filtration vacuum that doesn't fill the air with the pollutants it sucks from the carpet.

♦ If pet soiling is a problem, restrict pets to an uncarpeted area of the house if possible.

RECOMMENDED PRODUCTS:

♦ *Lindhaus PRO HEPA* upright and *Eureka OXYGEN* canister vacuums, both with HEPA filtration, offer the best value in performance, weight, quality & price.

These are available from the
Home Environment Center.
To order, call 1-888-612-5798
or visit www.YourHealthyHome.com.

♦ Hendericksen Naturlich Flooring
Phone: 707-829-3959

♦ Nature's Carpet
Phone: 206-682-7332
Web site: www.envirosource.com

RESOURCES:

The Carpet and Rug Institute
P.O. Box 2048
Dalton, GA 30722-2048
Phone: 800-882-8846
Web site: www.carpet-rug.com

– 5 –
Mold

- - - *NEWS FLASH* - - -

Family Members Suffer Permanent Brain Damage!
Million Dollar Home Must be Demolished!
Infant Admitted to Local Hospital with
Hemorrhaging in Lungs!

Seeing headlines like these you might think there was a serious chemical spill or even a nearby radiation leak or who knows what kind of disaster. Would you have ever suspected that a common mold was growing unnoticed somewhere in these homes?

On one hand, molds are a very necessary part of our ecosystem, as they contribute to biological decay and return basic nutrients to the earth. On the other hand, high mold levels indoors can have a <u>profoundly</u> negative effect on the building's occupants, especially more susceptible individuals.

Many of the people I talk to know they have an area in the house where mold is growing. They can <u>see</u> it. Others suspect they may have mold because of odor, symptoms and/or an area that stays wet all of the time.

Indoor mold can be one of the most insidious, potentially devastating indoor environmental risks we face. Mold can wreak havoc with every part of your body and your mind as well. Many symptoms of ill health, physical <u>and</u> mental, can result from ongoing exposure to high levels of harmful molds growing indoors in dry climates as well as more humid areas. Symptoms usually develop gradually and are very often vague, non-specific, difficult to diagnose and sufferers report laundry lists of complaints. Interestingly, a person living in a moldy environment may not always test positive for mold allergy.

If you suspect mold is a problem in your home but aren't certain, first thoroughly inspect every place in the house where water is used – around showers, dishwasher, washing machine, all sinks, water heater, air conditioner drain, behind the refrigerator, etc. for moisture (minor and major). If you don't have an obvious problem area, pay particular attention to closets that share a wall with a bath or laundry room. Textured ceilings also grow mold very quickly with a little moisture. Look for stains indicating roof leaks.

In many areas homes have basements that are wet all the time and are therefore moldy all the time. Please realize everything in a moldy basement is covered with mold and when you bring these things upstairs into your living area the mold comes with them, contributing to the overall mold activity in your home.

If you suspect mold is a problem you can also have your home tested. If your doctor or allergist doesn't know an industrial hygienist, check your yellow pages under Industrial Hygiene Consultants. If you find no listing in your area, call your nearest University Medical Center's Department of Environmental Medicine or contact the *American Industrial Hygiene Association.*

If you opt for testing, keep in mind that scientists deal in *"proven dose-response"* application of test results. For instance, below a certain concentration or dose there may be no scientific evidence of symptoms in a group of test subjects. However, you may be a more susceptible individual and may well become quite ill after prolonged exposure to lower levels or concentrations.

Please understand the following:

1) Any and all visible mold should be considered a <u>serious</u> health risk. It should be eliminated immediately and the cause of the growth, usually moisture, should be resolved.

2) The longer the exposure and the greater the dose (larger affected areas produce a greater number of spores), the higher your risk of serious health problems.

3) If your mold allergy test is negative, it doesn't change the importance of items 1 & 2.

4) Just because you don't see active mold growth doesn't mean you don't have high levels of airborne mold.

5) Living in a dry climate doesn't mean you have no risk for mold exposure.

6) If one member of the family is ill and none of the others are it doesn't mean you can rule out mold. Susceptibility and exposure times often vary from person to person.

CASE STORY: Bill, a retired President of a Fortune 100 company, came to see me on the recommendation of his son, already a client of mine. Bill told me that following his 76th birthday he had, for the first time in his life, developed serious allergies for no apparent reason. I asked Bill what had changed in his life and he said "absolutely nothing." I told him I suspected something had changed and proceeded to use the questionnaire on page 90 to further explore possible changes.

Bill said "no" to every question until I asked about water leaks. He then told me about the burst hose on the washing machine that filled the house with water. When I asked him where they found mold growing his first response was "when we pulled my bed away from the wall the shape of the headboard was left like a black shadow of mold on the wall."

I told Bill that was certainly a significant change in his life and a thorough restoration and elimination of the mold had to be done before it spread further. Furthermore, I told him I personally would not spend any time in the house until the work was finished. Fortunately, Bill and his wife were ready to leave for the summer anyway. Incidentally, Bill's wife's symptoms were apparently still ignorable even though his were quite serious.

CASE STORY: A local radio talk show host came to see me with a story of nearly a year-long search for answers to a multitude of health problems. Numerous tests, several different medications and, most recently, exploratory surgery. (He showed me the scar at the base of his throat.) Still no diagnosis and his condition was worsening!

When I asked how serious the water leak was in his house his mouth fell open and he wanted to know how I knew about the water leak. Just a lucky guess, I suppose. He went on to tell me of visible mold in every room. I recommended the same cleanup as in Bill's case and had him put an air purifier in the house. The whole family was quite pleased with the difference in a matter of days.

Mold Cleanup

It is very important that the cleanup of a moldy area be done properly. For instance, a very common mold problem can involve growth in a wall, in and under the carpet and on the slab or floor under the carpet. As soon as you disturb the area you cause a multitude of additional spores to be projected into the air. These spores are then distributed throughout the house and the likelihood of a widespread problem is increased.

When a mold remediation (cleanup and restoration) of any size is necessary, have professionals do the work if possible. If you choose to do the work yourself, please pay careful attention to the following:

1) First and foremost, protect yourself by wearing a safety suit and appropriate eye and breathing protection. Most cities have safety equipment suppliers listed in the yellow pages. Tell them what you are doing and ask them to recommend the right protection for the job.

2) When one room is being worked on, seal it off from the rest of the house. After opening a window, close and seal the door. Then seal the heating and cooling vents to prevent additional airborne spores from entering your HVAC system.

3) As the damaged materials are removed they should be sealed in plastic bags and placed outside through the open window (if the room is on the ground floor). Larger pieces that won't fit in bags should be handled separately and passed out through the window. Carrying these items through the house could further contaminate the rest of the house and should definitely be avoided.

4) The paper cover on both sides of sheetrock is a very willing host for mold. If a wall has been wet a number of times or remained wet for more than a few days the affected wall board should be removed and the interior of the wall cleaned and the mold killed before installing new sheetrock.

5) To kill mold some people use Borax or vinegar while others prefer a little bleach in a bucket of water. Some enzyme cleaners are also effective for this. The mold <u>must</u> be killed before the wall is closed and the floor is recovered.

Please remember, clothing, shoes, tools and even hair can become contaminated and then spread mold throughout the house. Once again, if at all possible, it is best to leave this work to professionals.

Humidity and Mold

The experts on mold agree that 55-60% humidity is the threshold above which mold growth can be a problem. As a homeowner you should keep in mind that even in the desert with 9% humidity mold can still be a problem indoors.

One of my clients in Tucson was having numerous health problems and, after a number of tests, was scheduled for a MRI, which provided no explanation for his symptoms. He was at first convinced he had no mold in his house. It turned out his shower was leaking water into the wall behind his bedroom closet. When he investigated the areas kept moist by the shower leak he found mold under the carpet, in the wall and under all the dresser drawers. In addition to the leak, he also had an evaporative cooler on the house. The increased humidity created by the cooler was further encouraging mold growth throughout the house.

Dry Climates

I quite often find humidifiers being used in dry climates. It's important to know that anytime you increase humidity you encourage mold growth. Secondly, humidifiers are seldom maintained as well as they should be, resulting in mold and/or bacteria growth in the humidifier that is then spread through the house. If you do have humidifiers, be certain to maintain them properly.

I have found that a number of my clients who have used humidifiers in the past are even happier without them once they put an air purifier in the house.

Wet Climates

In high humidity areas dehumidifiers can be helpful if, once again, they are maintained properly. I would also keep closet dryers (desiccant domes) in all of the closets to reduce moisture.

Basements are often problematic in regard to mold. Some basements are wet all the time with no practical way to prevent the wetness. In the case of a wet, moldy basement, do your best to seal the separation between the basement and the rest of the house to reduce the transfer of mold into the living areas. You can also run an ozone generator in your basement while it's unoccupied to curtail mold growth and freshen the air.

House Plants

Another source of mold indoors is the potting soil for your houseplants. As much as I enjoy green plants in the house, I try to limit their number, keep from over-watering those I do have and avoid the additional mold. You may have heard of people claiming to purify indoor air with living plants. Sorry! It would take so many to make a significant difference in air quality there would be no room for anything else and the resultant molds would be seriously detrimental!

I hope by now you realize that mold is nothing to take lightly. If you have visible mold in your home I would deal with it <u>immediately</u>.

RECOMMENDATIONS:
- Resolve any leaks and sources of indoor moisture immediately. The longer things stay wet, the more difficulty and expense you will have.
- Thoroughly remove and clean up any visible mold.
- Even minor roof leaks should be repaired immediately.
- If your washing machine hoses are five or more years old, replace them. Don't wait for them to fail and fill your house with water and the resultant mold.
- If your water heater is indoors and twenty or more years old, don't wait for it to fail, replace it NOW.

- Purify your indoor air. My preference is a *filterless,* whole-house electronic air purifier.
- Use an ozone generator in the basement to control mold.
- Avoid evaporative coolers. Use air conditioning whenever possible.
- Use desiccant domes in closets. Limit use of humidifiers and be diligent in their maintenance if you do use them.
- In damp climates, use dehumidifiers to reduce humidity.

RECOMMENDED PRODUCTS:

- *Living Air* (**whole house air purifiers**) manufactures a line of portable, *filterless,* electronic air purifiers designed to clean the air in your entire house, eliminating odors from pets, smoke, cooking, new paint and carpet, mold and mildew, while also settling particles from the air. **One unit** will produce **fresher, cleaner, healthier air** in every room of the house.
- *The Com Air Blaster* (**ozone generator**) is very useful for controlling mold activity in basements. The integral timer provides for periodic production of ozone at levels that will kill mold.
- *The Companion Electrostatic Filter* for your air conditioning unit / furnace is washable & reusable. It's a layered fabric filter that captures particles using static attraction.
- **Desiccant domes** to reduce humidity in confined spaces. **The** *Dri Out Dome* is a good one.
- *Your Healthy Home Mold Test Kit* gives you a simple, inexpensive way to do a basic mold activity test in your home.

**The products listed above are all available from the
Home Environment Center.
To order call 1-888-612-5798
or visit www.YourHealthyHome.com.**

ADDITIONAL INFORMATION:

Is This Your Child? Dr. Doris Rapp
(ISBN 0-688-11907-7)

Thriving in a Toxic World Dr. William R. Kellas
(ISBN 0-963-64911-6 / ISBN 0-963-64912-4)

An Alternative Approach to Allergy Dr. Theron Randolph
(ISBN 0-553-20830-6)

– 6 –
Heating and Cooling Systems

Let's begin with a discussion of existing systems and what you need to know to maintain your healthy home's heating and cooling system. If you only learn one thing from this chapter I'd like it to be the lesson illustrated by the following case story.

> *CASE STORY:* Joe and Elsa had been married for decades, living together in a little house they bought in 1951. However, in '94 they decided to live apart and Joe moved out. One day that winter their long time neighbor and friend discovered Elsa had died in her sleep. Shortly thereafter Joe moved back into the house and the following winter Joe *also* died.
>
> When I inspected the furnace I found it to be the original 1951 gas furnace with a hole in the heat exchanger large enough for my thumb to pass through. Even a <u>cracked</u> heat exchanger could have filled the house with carbon monoxide (CO)! It's very possible they both sought medical treatment for any number of difficult to diagnose symptoms with no diagnosis. I'd say it's also likely no one asked about their house and so the massive CO leak went undetected.

The moral to this story: Please don't let anyone you care about (or yourself) live in a house with a gas furnace without having it cleaned and inspected annually by someone who knows what they're doing. And don't wait for the first hard freeze or snow storm. Call your heating/ cooling service person before their peak season hits so you're ready to go when it gets cold.

If you suspect a gas or carbon monoxide (CO) leak, call your local gas company. They will usually respond within hours to check for leaks (normally for free). It is also critical, in my opinion, that you have at least one CO detector near your bedrooms. And, of course, smoke/fire alarms are an absolute necessity. Please don't forget to regularly service battery powered units. These devices save lives every day.

Central System Filters

Over the past several years a number of new central system filters have been introduced. We now have electronic, electrostatic, HEPA, pleated paper and the same old $2.00 - $3.00 fiberglass filters available. You may be surprised to learn that filters were originally designed into air conditioners and furnaces to protect the equipment and minimize fire risk, <u>not</u> to filter the air we breathe. The better filters will remove *large* particles that actually make their way to the cold air return but <u>they do not</u> address the vast majority of the air we breathe and the smallest airborne particles and gasses in our homes.

Please remember that once or twice a year isn't often enough to service your filter, especially if you have indoor pets. Not only does the accumulation on the filter create an added load on the blower motor, <u>it also provides a very effective breeding ground for mold and bacteria</u>. A 30-60 day cleaning schedule is best.

Most of the systems in people's homes use the 1 inch thick filter and for those applications I prefer an electrostatic air filter. The layers of fabric have coatings that create an electrostatic attraction to the fabric as air passes through it. No electrical connections are needed and the filter is washed with water every 30-60 days.

Central System Ducts

CASE STORY: I recently had a call from a friend in Illinois regarding a friend of hers who, along with her daughter, had been sick ever since they moved into their home. Her question had to do with the dark streaks on the walls around the supply registers in her house. She wanted to know what they might be. We've all seen this blackening around registers and it could be any number of things including:

   ♦   Exhaust from combustion (in the case of a gas furnace)

- Mold growing in the duct system

- Dirt, insulation material and who knows what else entering the ducts through leaky duct joints in the attic or crawl space

And which of these should be blowing around in *your* healthy home? None of the above, of course! Do not delay in a case like this. It is entirely possible that people in this home will get progressively sicker if the central system is in fact causing their difficulty. Remember, a hotel in Philadelphia put *Legionnaire's Disease* on the map as a result of the bacteria *(Legionella)* growing in the duct work.

So, what should you <u>DO</u>?

1. Have a professional inspect and service the furnace. Any reputable, licensed heating/cooling contractor will do. If you don't know one, ask a friend for a referral.

2. Have the ducts leak tested (& sealed if necessary) and cleaned. My preferred duct cleaning approach is provided by *Video-Aire*. Their service includes before and after video taping of your ducts so you have clear proof of what was there before and after. The antimicrobial treatment of the ducts is optional. If you are sensitive or allergic, discuss this part of the process with the operator before work begins.

Condensation Drains

Air conditioning systems all condense moisture and collect the water in a tray that drains to the outside. Condensation leaks are quite common and can cause mold growth in the return plenum that then blows all through the house. Any leak in this area should be repaired as soon as possible. *(See also Chapter 5 on Mold.)*

New Construction

It's hard to argue with the efficiency and performance of forced air gas heat. However, from the standpoint of a healthier alternative, radiant or electric heat — if these systems are practical in your area — should be considered.

Evaporative Cooling

In drier climates quite a few homes are still equipped with evaporative (swamp) coolers. These coolers can be a constant source of difficulty for allergic / sensitive people. They not only bring outdoor pollen, mold and pollution into the house but also raise the humidity and encourage indoor mold growth. Avoid evaporative coolers whenever possible, opting for zoned air conditioning with sufficient insulation to minimize electrical costs as an alternative.

RECOMMENDATIONS:

♦ Avoid using liquid or solid fuel-burning heaters unless they are properly vented to the outside and ventilate the house as well. Even then, I prefer to avoid them.

♦ When using fireplaces or wood-burning stoves, make certain the chimney is drafting properly to prevent smoke and chemicals from accumulating indoors. Avoid burning manufactured logs that contain glues and/or petroleum products. Also avoid burning trash, painted wood scraps, plastic and wrapping paper during the holidays as they can produce toxic gasses when burned.

♦ Avoid air conditioning and heater ducting with fiberglass insulation inside the duct. Not only can loose fibers be blown into the air but their porosity provides a place for mold, bacteria and odors to develop.

RECOMMENDED PRODUCTS:

Contact a professional local heating and cooling contractor for quality, recommended systems suited to your house and climate.

RESOURCES:

♦ *Video-Aire International* (duct cleaning)
Call 888-494-1711 for an operator in your area.

ADDITIONAL INFORMATION:

The Household Environment and Chronic Illness Guy Pfeiffer
Residential Space Heating Tricia Hutchcraft

– 7 –
Water

Let's talk first about water for human consumption. The quality of the water you drink and cook with is the most critical.

Harmful Microorganisms

The most serious short-term health risk comes from harmful microorganisms in drinking water, i.e. bacteria, cysts, viruses. One day in 1993 in Milwaukee, the hospital emergency rooms began to fill with people, all suffering from similar symptoms. By the time the cause was discovered 400,000 were ill and over 100 people eventually died. A cyst called cryptosporidium had somehow spread throughout the city's water supply. "Crypto" is not susceptible to the chlorine in municipal water supplies. Fortunately, this bug doesn't show up very often, but that didn't help the city of Milwaukee.

Many experts believe stomach flus and many other contagions are also transferred via municipal water systems. Municipal water supplies are regularly monitored for bacteria and most cities use chlorine and/or ozone to control bacteria. But, and this is a BIG "but," you don't know what can show up in tap water from one minute to the next.

One day people in Pineville, Louisiana, noticed something white and stringy coming out of their faucets. They soon realized it was toilet paper. Someone at the water utility had made a mistake and temporarily introduced *raw sewage* into the water supply!

Just yesterday the water at our taps was "safe" and today it could be deadly. Ask the people in Alpine, Wyoming, or Walkerton, Ontario, who experienced

E-coli contaminated water. People died from drinking a glass of water because an animal had fallen into a well and died.

In defense of the water utilities, do you understand the enormity of their job? Taking surface waters and water from wells and delivering it through millions of miles of pipe all over the country, they have to make it "safe" to drink. Accidents will happen and mistakes will be made. Therefore, I believe it is critical that we control the safety of our water in our own homes to be <u>certain</u> we have healthy water for our families.

Other Bacteria Sources

It is important to note two common <u>in-home</u> sources of bacteria in residential water: filters on refrigerator water lines and whole house softeners. The filter on the refrigerator should be changed EVERY SIX MONTHS in most cases, certainly never less than once per year. Likewise, whole house water softeners can sometimes develop a bacterial growth if not properly maintained.

Bottom Line

If an odor or taste has developed in your water, or someone in the house is having unexplained health problems, do a bacteria test. If there is harmful bacteria present, identify its source and sanitize the plumbing in the house to eliminate it.

Nitrates

Nitrates may occur in any well but are most commonly found in shallow wells. Well water may contain nitrates as a result of contact with nitrate-bearing minerals in soil. It may also result from the presence of certain fertilizers and/or human or animal waste.

In concentrations as low as 10-20 parts per million, nitrates have been connected with illness and even death among infants under six months of age.

A simple test will reveal any nitrates in your water. If your water contains nitrates, your best source of help is a local water treatment professional familiar with water quality issues in your area.

Lead

While not as lethal as harmful microorganisms, lead in drinking water can have a devastating effect over time. Childhood exposure to lead (as well as other heavy metals) can cause learning disabilities, impaired reading ability and poor eye/hand coordination.

If your area was developed or your home was built over 25 years ago I suggest you test your water for lead. In-home test kits are inexpensive and simple to use.

What About Private Wells?

CASE STORY: Several years ago I heard of a woman who had been chronically ill with a laundry list of "undiagnosable" symptoms for years. She had made the rounds of all the even remotely related specialties in medicine. She was finally referred to a psychiatrist (sound familiar?) because *"there just wasn't any physical reason for her 'illness'."* Her problems continued and one day she went to see a chiropractor. After hearing her history and reviewing her records, the doctor asked where she got her drinking water. She said her family had their own well on the property.

A simple test revealed salmonella bacteria in the well. It turned out that uphill from them was a neighbor with a chicken coop. Some of the run-off from his place was finding its way into her well. The rest of her family hadn't been affected enough to cause them to seek treatment but she was so susceptible as to be debilitated for years.

For private wells, there is an in-home bacteria test kit available for $20 or less. Many testing laboratories will also do a bacteria test for about $35.00. One way or another, test your well water at least once a year just to be sure. Your local water treatment professionals can help with well sanitizing if necessary.

What About the REST of the Stuff in Drinking Water?

Water testing is routinely done free of charge by water treatment dealers across the country. They generally test for iron, pH (acidity), nitrates, chlorine, hardness and dissolved solids. In some areas volatile organic compounds (VOCs) can be a problem. For instance, in southwest Tucson, Arizona, trichlorethylene (TCE) from a defense plant found its way into the aquifer in a sufficient amount to cause a multimillion dollar clean-up and closing of certain wells.

There is a very long list of other contaminants found in our water supplies. Some are on the list of regulated contaminants and others are unregulated. MTBE (methyl-t-butyl-ether) has been the subject of numerous news stories recently. It has also been added to the "contaminant candidate list" for further evaluation and possible regulation. MTBE is a fuel oxygenate that has been used since 1979 to replace lead as an octane enhancer. Its presence in water has been linked to leaking underground fuel tanks, spills and the settling of auto exhaust from the air.

EPA has said they find it unlikely that any negative health effects would result from concentrations below 40 ppb (parts per billion) in drinking water. The first major water contamination incident that brought attention to MTBE was in Santa Monica, California, in 1996. They discovered MTBE in two wellfields at concentrations of 610 ppb in one field and 86 ppb in the other. Both fields were closed and water was purchased from neighboring water utilities.

Keep in mind, any water test you do is just a snapshot in time. It will tell you what was present at the time you collected the sample. Conditions can and do change from time to time. Most people with an interest in living a healthy lifestyle stopped drinking untreated tap water years ago. Many others now consider an in-home water treatment system a necessity.

In most situations I prefer the *Living Water*™ UV / ozone / filter system for drinking water purification. The *Living Water*™ produces great tasting water and protects against bacteria and cysts (like giardia and cryptosporidium), volatile organic chemicals (VOCs) and removes particles 1 micron or larger.

Reverse Osmosis (R.O.) is another popular treatment method. R.O. Systems produce water slowly using nano-filtration and accumulate the purified water in a tank under the sink.

NOTE: It is important to perform the necessary maintenance with any water system. If you move into a home with an existing water system, immediately determine if it is due for maintenance. If documentation of the last service isn't available, go ahead and do a filter change and sanitize the system so you know it's done!

If an in-home system isn't possible, the next best thing is to buy purified water by the gallon. Most water stores charge between 25 and 45 cents per gallon. Make certain your bottles are clean (free of bacteria) before filling. The best water stores will sanitize your bottles with ozonated water sprayed under pressure into your inverted bottles prior to filling them.

Water for Bathing and Laundry

CASE STORY: One of our clients, an automotive engineer from Dearborn, Michigan, called one day to order a shower filter. Two weeks later he called to tell us why he wanted it. He had a box full of soaps that he had tried one after another in an effort to solve a very annoying skin problem. After installing the shower filter he once again used each of the bars of soap and now, not a single one bothered him! He called to tell us it was the water that caused his problem and the filter solved it.

Some people react on contact to *something* in tap water. Others react to the *soap residue and dirt* left in clothes that are washed in hard water. The water treatment industry does an amazing demonstration by putting a freshly laundered (in hard water) baby's night shirt or wash cloth in a bowl of soft water. Just a couple of squeezes and the water turns dark and foamy from the residue left in the fabric! I wonder how many heat rashes are caused by this caustic residue. The harder the water, the more residue is retained in the fabric.

Tucson, Arizona, is intending to "blend" their existing ground water with Colorado River water and increase the hardness from seven grains per gallon to *seventeen* grains per gallon: a windfall for local dermatologists! Many people who have never had skin problems will develop them as a result of this harder water and additional chemicals.

But wait, there's more!

When you bathe or shower in warm water your skin pores open and absorb more and by heating and aerosolizing the water you increase the volatility of the chlorine and other VOC's in the water. While you are showering, what else do you do? You *breathe*, of course, and inhale these pollutants into your lungs where they are absorbed directly into your bloodstream.

A number of studies have shown that several times as much chlorine ends up in your bloodstream when you take a shower as when you drink the same water. Unless you have a whole house system for chlorine removal, use a filter on each shower head. Shower filters are available in handheld as well as wall-mounted styles, with or without shower massage heads. Both work great and have replaceable filter cartridges.

It is best to treat the water as it comes into the house by softening / sequestering and removing the chlorine at that point. Softening removes minerals or "hardness" from the water. Sequestering provides the benefits of soft water by holding these same minerals or "hardness" in suspension, eliminates the need for salt or potassium and doesn't waste any water. There are many additional benefits to sequestered water including cleaner clothes, less shower scale, preservation of plumbing fixtures, dishwasher, water heater and washing machine as well as conservation of soap and shampoo.

As you can see, there are many issues involved with water quality and entire books have been written on water alone.

A final word to the wise . . .

Never, ever drink water or eat loose ice from inside an ice chest. Some very nasty "bugs" grow in ice chests! When you store an ice chest, prop the lid open so air can move in and out and wash it before each use.

RECOMMENDATIONS:
For local water testing, consult your Yellow Pages for a testing laboratory in your area.

RECOMMENDED PRODUCTS:
♦ For drinking water, the *Living Water*™ system combines the natural benefits of ultraviolet light and ozone injection with a 1 micron carbon filter. This is

an excellent, affordable way to protect against harmful microorganisms and volatile organic chemicals. The *Living Water*™ is compact, easy to install and produces great tasting water.

◆ For whole house water treatment, the *Spring House*™ system is my choice in most cases. Combining sequestration (for the benefits of soft water without salt or potassium) with five stages of filtration and ultraviolet light, the *Spring House*™ gives you drinking-quality water throughout the house.

◆ The *Living Water all-in-one Showerheads*™ will remove the effects of chlorine and other chemical toxins from your water. You'll notice you're using less soap and shampoo and your hair and skin will feel great. Wall mounted and hand held models are available.

◆ *YourHealthy Home Water Test Kits* for bacteria, chlorine, hardness, nitrates, nitrites, ph, sulphur, iron and lead are available for easy testing by homeowners.

**The products listed above are all available from the
Home Environment Center.
To order, call 1-888-612-5798
or visit www.YourHealthyHome.com.**

RESOURCES:

Environmental Protection Agency
Safe Drinking Water Hotline
Phone: 800-426-4791
Web site: www.epa.gov

Water Quality Association
4151 Naperville Rd.
Lisle, IL 60532
Phone: 708-505-0160
Web site: www.wqa.org

National Sanitation Foundation
789 N. Dixboro Road
Ann Arbor, MI 48113-0140
Phone: 877-867-3435
Web site: www.nsf.org

– 8 –
Building Materials

"We shape our dwellings and afterwards our dwellings shape our lives."
Winston Churchill

In 1991 my wife and I decided to have a custom home built. We purchased a lot and hired a general contractor to build our new home. I was still quite sensitive to chemicals and knew I would have to do considerable research on building materials before we began construction. Every time we saw a house being built we would stop and study the building materials being used as we gathered information and I experienced exposure to various materials and products. We contacted manufacturers to learn about the ingredients in their products and decided we wanted:

1) Only low VOC paints and finishes. (Today, <u>ZERO</u> VOC paints are available.) This meant no oil-based finishes indoors.

2) No particle board inside. We used solid wood cabinets.

3) Only *Murco* brand drywall joint compound used on the walls, because most other brands contain mildewcides and/or formaldehyde to which I and many people are reactive.

4) Part ceramic tile and part carpet on the floors. We avoided petroleum-based sealers on the grout and adhesives under the carpet pad. (*The Carpet and Rug Institute* now rates floor covering products for their outgassing potential.)

5) Roof vents and screened air intake vents in the garage to prevent

pressure buildup that might force air from that area into our living area and also to provide ventilation of odors and gasses.

6) No sprayed foam insulation in the walls or ceilings.

Our builder was very cooperative regarding our requirements for healthy materials in our home, although I could tell he thought we were hypochondriacs or lunatics or both. He did a great job for us and our healthy home was just what we had hoped it would be – a pleasant, healthy environment that caused us no noticeable adverse health effects.

CASE STORY: As you know, life is full of surprises. One day, about six years after he built our home, I ran into our builder and heard an all too familiar story. Bob told me how he had difficulty taking me seriously regarding our building materials when our home was under construction. Since then, however, he had learned to take these issues very seriously.

Bob had been very fit and athletic all his life and was virtually free of health problems until one day he walked into a home he was building. His chest got tight, he was struggling for each breath, collapsed on the floor, and was taken by ambulance to the Emergency Room that day. He has needed to make that same trip 3 more times! Since he is now reactive to many materials he formerly worked with, he continues to have difficulty going into homes under construction if the materials are not carefully chosen.

Just because you're *not* sick (reactive, allergic, sensitive) today doesn't mean you won't be tomorrow. Many materials outgas for extended periods of time, and sensitivities can develop with long-term exposure. Susceptible individuals can experience symptoms even after the odors are not detectable by most people.

CASE STORY: I recently walked into a professional office and experienced an immediate reaction to the joint compound on the interior walls. This office had been painted, furnished and occupied for at least a couple of months. Still, it was clear to me that something other than *Murco* joint compound had been used to coat and texture the walls. I could smell the all too familiar chemical odor and feel the tightness in my throat and irritation to my sinuses.

As I spoke with the people working in this office, I learned of headaches, fatigue, "spaciness," etc. from some, though not all, of the occupants. Others just objected to the smell. If all the materials for this office had been chosen more wisely, it is likely that few, if any of these problems would have occurred. It was, of course, totally impractical to tear out the offending materials; so, I assisted them in choosing an air purifier, which we placed on a bookcase in the center of the office. Within a couple of days the air smelled fresh and clean and everyone was thrilled with the effect.

To illustrate how common this problem is in homes and offices we have only to look at the *Environmental Protection Agency.* The EPA's own building in Washington DC was a sick building to begin with, full of mold, rodent waste, pesticides, etc. But, after they installed new carpet and furniture we saw their employees on national television picketing the agency in front of their own building. The picket signs read *"Your Building is Killing Us!"* It was reported that some of these people suffered long term illness as a result of this exposure while others were affected only temporarily.

Lead-based Paints

Some older homes contain lead-based paints and small children may ingest some of this paint if it is exposed. If you have a concern, *Your Healthy Home Lead Test* will identify paint that contains lead. It is important to note that lead-based paints in older homes are generally considered safe if they've been painted over and aren't chipped or peeling.

Please remember, everything we bring into our living and working environments has the potential to cause us difficulty. Individual reactivity depends on many factors including each person's susceptibility to the offending agent(s). Here again, entire books have been written on this topic. For more detailed information on building materials and practices, please reference the following sources.

RECOMMENDED PRODUCTS:

Murco Wall Products (Drywall Joint Compound)
300 N. E. 21st Street
Fort Worth, Texas 76106
Phone: 817-626-1987
Fax: 817-626-0821
Web site: www.angelfire.lycos.com/tx/Murco

Dunn Edwards Paint Corp. (Zero VOC Paint)
4885 E. 52nd Place
Los Angeles, CA 90040
Phone: 888) DE-PAINT (888-337-2468)
Web site: www.dunnedwards.com

Pace Industries, Inc. (Particle Board Sealer)
779 S. LaGrange Ave.
Newbury Park, CA 91320
Phone: 805-499-2911

Air-Krete, Inc. (Insulation)
P.O. Box 380
Weedsport, NY 13166-0380
Phone: 315-834-6609 phone/fax
Web site: www.airkrete.com

RESOURCES:

The Carpet and Rug Institute
P.O. Box 2048
Dalton, GA 30722-2048
Phone: 800-882-8846 1-800-882-8846
Web site: www.carpet-rug.com

ADDITIONAL INFORMATION:

Surviving the Toxic Crisis Dr. William R. Kellas
(ISBN 0-963-64911-6 / ISBN 0-963-64912-4)

The Household Environment and Chronic Illness Guy Pfeiffer

– 9 –
Pest Control

How many people do you suppose actually <u>read</u> the warning labels on pest control packages?

CASE STORY: Last year I was an exhibitor at a chiropractic convention. One of the doctors I met there told me of a problem she and her family were having. Incidentally, her husband is also a doctor. It seemed for the past year and a half they had all experienced far more illness than usual, including new allergies, frequent colds, etc. She was concerned that dust was her problem and wanted to know if our air purifier would help. I suggested that she try one and see for herself. After a week she called to say they felt no better and I should come by her office and pick up the purifier.

When I met with her at her office, she pointed at the purifier and commented on the amount of dust on it. It didn't appear to me to be a lot of dust for one week's use.

After one week's use, in a typical home, I would expect a light accumulation of dust. However, the <u>inside</u> of this unit was solid white and so sticky I had to use a paper towel to free my fingers from the goo. I said, "Doctor, your problem isn't dust, it's <u>chemical</u>." She was immediately defensive, saying she had no chemicals in her house.

As I quizzed her about all the possible sources of this volume of chemical she said no to every item until I said "moth balls." She then told me of a problem they had experienced with moths a year and a half earlier. She put moth balls under the beds, in the dresser drawers and in the closets in an effort to control the moths. When I asked her if she had read the warning on the package she said she knew all of "these kinds of products" had a standard warning. The color drained from her face when I told her <u>this</u> warning was far more serious because it says *"May be fatal if inhaled."* I have reproduced that label here so you can see for yourself.

WARNING: KEEP OUT OF REACH OF CHILDREN – SEE BACK PANEL FOR ADDITIONAL PRECAUTIONS. MAY BE FATAL IF INHALED. HARMFUL IF SWALLOWED. AVOID BREATHING VAPORS OR DUST. AVOID CONTACT WITH SKIN, EYES OR CLOTHING.

CASE STORY: Within a few weeks of the above experience I went with my plumber to install a drinking water system for a retired couple. Walking through the door I was immediately aware of the unmistakable odor of mothballs. Our discussion revealed that the water system was being purchased because of the wife's long-standing chronic illness. Her doctors had instructed her to drink only purified water. As we talked further, I learned that she had been ill for many years and they had also scattered moth balls about their homes for many years.

I wouldn't presume to blame this woman's illness entirely on moth balls, but I am convinced they played a significant role. Her husband, a retired chemistry professor, still wonders why it didn't occur to *him* sooner to get rid of the moth balls. As effective as cedar is, I don't know why anyone would use mothballs anyway!

Okay, enough moth ball stories.

Obviously, moths are only one of many pests for which there are numerous pesticides available, specially formulated for indoor and outdoor use. I personally choose not to use any pesticides indoors that are *sprayed.* I do put out an occasional ant bait or roach trap but primarily rely on electronic insect repellers such as those available from *Lentek International* for indoor protection. Their extensive line of products does a great job on most of the common indoor pests, including mosquitoes. They use sound and energy (undetectable by humans and pets) to drive out unwanted pests.

Outdoor Chemicals Found To Be More Concentrated Indoors Than Out!

A recent EPA study of a household of four with a dog found diazanon levels in their indoor air and carpet *50 times higher than outside levels.* This research at EPA's National Exposure Research Lab in North Carolina was comparing the levels of pesticides in newly treated lawns with indoor levels. The family dog is getting much of the blame since the pesticide concentration on his paws was found to be as much as <u>250 times greater</u> than the levels in the yard. *(See also Chapter 10 on House Pets.)* Many of these lawn and garden chemicals work by attacking the nervous system of the insects. It comes as no surprise to me that scientific studies have already linked certain pesticide exposures with Parkinson's Disease and many experts suspect a connection with other neurological problems. I believe we are all well advised to limit our exposure to these chemicals.

If you <u>do</u> use chemical pesticides, *remember* ... the warnings and directions are there for a reason. Don't get creative. If you use these products at all, use them <u>exactly</u> as directed on the label.

And finally, while one of the most effective things you can do to prevent insect problems is maintain a clean house, you may still have some difficulty with pests. For example, in the Southwest we have a problem with kissing bugs. This little blood sucking parasite lives and feeds on the cute kangaroo rats (like ground squirrels) that nest in the desert around our homes. The kissing bugs sometimes leave the rats' nests and make their way into a house and feed on humans. Their bite causes painful, itchy swelling and can even throw sensitized individuals into anaphylactic shock.

Obviously, preventing wild creatures from setting up housekeeping too near your house can also reduce the likelihood of their pests coming indoors, so I suggest keeping a clean yard as well. Since I removed all of the rats' nests within thirty feet of our house six years ago we haven't seen a single kissing bug.

Pest infestations in attics, walls and crawl spaces can also present a serious health risk. Bats, bees, birds, insects and rodents along with their prey and waste should not be allowed to accumulate anywhere in the structure. Clean out any debris and close all openings to prevent future problems.

Caution! Anytime you undertake an outdoor project of this type, be certain to wear effective breathing protection and skin coverage. You don't want to inhale these pollutants into your lungs or, heaven forbid, be the next Hanta Virus case. Likewise, when spraying pesticides and herbicides outdoors, wear appropriate protection and clean those articles of clothing separately from the rest of your laundry. And, of course, store these chemicals safely and clean up your spray equipment according to label directions. Better yet, whenever possible, hire professionals to do the work and avoid the exposure altogether.

Termites

Prevention of termite infestations is, of course, the best approach and a few simple precautions can save a lot of expense and difficulty later.

1) Prevent wood (including firewood) or paper materials from accumulating near the exterior walls of the house.

2) Patch or seal any cracks in foundations or walls to close any easy points of entry.

3) Be sure that soil around the house is contoured to prevent water from standing against the foundation.

4) My current preference for termite treatment is underground termite baits that don't require soaking the foundation with chemicals.

Treatment methods vary from one area to another. This is another case where it pays to do your homework before allowing your home to be chemically treated.

Here again, we are making new discoveries all the time regarding the adverse health effects of chemicals commonly used in our living and work environments. For example, in early 2000 we saw new controls placed on *Dursban*, a chemical pesticide that was used for years and believed to be safe.

RECOMMENDED PRODUCTS:

♦ *Lentek International* makes an extensive line of electronic pest control devices that work well in most environments and eliminate the need for many chemicals. Their products are available from the *Home Environment Center* at 1-888-612-5798 or visit www.YourHealthyHome.com.

♦ *Bioganics* has formulated a selection of plant-based insecticides and herbicides that don't endanger humans, pets, fish or birds. *Bioganics* products are carried by Walmart, Home Depot, Lowe's and others, or contact them online at www.bioganic.com. For professional/agricultural products go to www.ecosmart.com.

RESOURCES:
National Coalition Against the Misuse of Pesticides
530 7th St. SE
Washington, DC 20003
Phone: 202-543-5450 / 1-800-882-8846
Web site: www.ncamp.org

ADDITIONAL INFORMATION:
Is This Your Child? Dr. Doris Rapp, MD
(ISBN 0-688-11907-7)

Thriving in a Toxic World Dr. William R. Kellas
(ISBN 0-963-64911-6 / ISBN 0-963-64912-4)

– 10 –
House Pets

As much as we love our pets, we can't deny they make their own contribution to pollution in our homes. If I only had a nickel . . . for every time I've heard a parent say *"My six year old has severe asthma and is highly allergic to cats but I just don't have the heart to tell her she can't sleep with her cat!"* This would be an easy choice for me, yet I know it isn't easy for everyone. Please keep in mind the importance of sleeping in the healthiest possible environment and consider its impact on your child's health.

Dander

The most widely recognized issue regarding pets is their dander. Here again, cats suffer a great deal of criticism largely due to the high percentage of people who are severely reactive to cat dander. Cats, however, are hardly alone when it comes to dander related allergy.

Dog dander can give certain people a great deal of difficulty too, as can bird dander and feathers. In the case of cats and dogs, frequent grooming, use of moisturizing shampoos and treating their coats with deionized water or one of the dander reducing coat treatments may help. A whole house air purifier will also help keep the air fresher and cleaner.

Pest Control

If you suffer symptoms when exposed to your pet, dander may not be to blame. You may be reacting to chemicals in a flea/tick collar or powders or shampoos. Pets can also develop parasite problems and/or carry them in from outside. With this in mind, are you sure you want your pet on the bed?

Outdoor Exposures

When your pet comes in from outside it also brings with it many of the outdoor pollutants: pesticides, vehicle and industrial pollution, bacteria, mold, pollen, etc. Therefore, frequent grooming and regular bathing are important.

Your New Home

Often I hear from families who suffer terrible reactions after they move into a pre-owned residence or apartment only to learn later that the prior owner had animals to which they are allergic. In many of these cases, the new residents are happy just purifying the air. For others a complete change of floor coverings, a thorough duct cleaning and wall scrubbing are necessary.

If pets, especially cats, have urinated into the carpets, the floor or slab is also contaminated and should be thoroughly cleaned. Enzyme or colloidal cleaners are very effective for this purpose and leave no chemical residue like chlorine or ammonia-based products do. Local restoration services should be able to help.

> *CASE STORY:* I recently heard of a home where a cat had sprayed into a floor register for the heating system. After numerous attempts to clean up the register and duct the odor was still <u>unbearable</u>. Fortunately for the homeowners, a brief application of ozone completely <u>eliminated</u> the odor.

RECOMMENDED PRODUCTS:

♦ *Living Air*™ manufactures a line of portable, *filterless,* **electronic air purifiers** designed to clean the air in your entire house, eliminating odors from pets, smoke, cooking, new paint and carpet, mold and mildew, while also settling particles from the air. *One unit* will produce *fresher, cleaner, healthier air* in every room of the house.

♦ *The Companion™ Electrostatic filter* for your air conditioning unit / furnace is washable & reusable. It's a layered fabric filter that captures particles using static attraction.

◆ *Dust mite / allergy proof pillows,* pillow covers, and mattress encasements to control mite activity.

The products listed above are all available from the Home Environment Center. To order, call 1-888-612-5798 or visit www.YourHealthyHome.com.

ADDITIONAL INFORMATION:
The Encyclopedia of Natural Pet Care C.J. Puotinen (ISBN 0-658-00996-6)

– 11 –
Electrical Fields

Here's a subject surrounded by controversy!

Do electrical fields really cause adverse health effects or not? The scientific community, for the most part, says <u>no</u>.

Would I regularly sleep or allow a child of mine to sleep in a 5 milligauss field? Certainly not! Would I live in a house within 500 yards of a major, overhead electrical power line? *No, thank you!* It's hard to know what may be discovered about this exposure 10 years from now. Common sense tells us if it doesn't cost anything to avoid the exposure, it is only prudent that we do so.

Following are some of the common household sources of electrical fields:

- **Electric ranges, TV's, refrigerators, ovens and microwaves** – While in operation these appliances create energy fields of varying intensity that pass through walls like they weren't even there.

- **Breaker box / electrical service** – Any time a major appliance or air conditioner runs there is a considerable field created around the breaker box. If your bed's headboard is on that wall, you are bathed in that field. If possible, move the bed to another wall.

- **Clock radios** – Some clock radios create a surprisingly strong field. I keep mine at least 4 feet from my head. Another alternative is to switch to a battery-powered alarm clock.

- **Computers** – The further you sit from the CRT, the better. Three feet or more is recommended.

- **Electric blankets and waterbed heaters** – If you use these, turn them on to warm the bed and turn them off while you sleep.

- **Cell phones** – Using an ear piece and microphone will keep the phone and its signal away from your head.

It's very possible the scientific experts may remain divided in their opinions. I'll just go ahead and err on the side of caution and suggest you do the same.

– 12 –
Lighting

When my wife and I first met, one of our early discoveries as we got to know each other was we had both installed full spectrum lighting in our offices. How many couples can say that?

Our experience with fluorescent lighting had been exactly the same. Working much of the day under fluorescent light we had experienced eye strain, fatigue, irritability, headaches, etc. Using the full spectrum bulbs and tubes that produce a quality of light almost identical to natural sunlight we both felt measurably better.

In his book *Thriving in a Toxic World*, Dr. William Kellas, Ph.D., writes, *"If the body doesn't get certain light wave lengths, it may not be able to fully absorb certain nutrients. Poor illumination can contribute to fatigue, depression, hostility, suppressed immune function, strokes, hair loss, skin damage, alcoholism, drug abuse, Alzheimer's disease and cancer. Poor light has also been linked to a loss of muscle tone and strength."* ... *"Exposure to full spectrum light has eased high blood pressure, depression, insomnia, PMS, migraines and carbohydrate craving."*

In the book, *Light Years Ahead*, Brian Breiling, Psy.D. and David Olszewski, EE, IE write, *"A research study showed that by simply switching the classroom lighting to full spectrum radiation-shielded fluorescents it decreased the hyperactive behavior of students compared to a control group. Similarly, when Control Data Corporation installed full spectrum fluorescent tubes in their work stations, the data input error rate dropped to the point of saving the company more than $235,000 per year."* ... *"The companies that use full spectrum light report employee morale has improved while complaints of headaches and eyestrain while working at video display terminals have greatly decreased."*

Healthy Home Lighting

The benefits of full spectrum light are widely documented. Likewise, the problems resulting from a lack of exposure to natural light are well known in northern regions where Seasonal Affective Disorder Syndrome (SADS) is a common problem. SADS sufferers often experience substantial improvement with daily exposure to full spectrum light. Many of these people simply sit in front of a full spectrum light box as they read, pay bills or write letters.

You don't have to live in a northern region to be affected by a lack of natural light exposure. Even people who live in southern climates who spend the majority of the daylight hours indoors report benefits when using full spectrum lighting.

Additional Benefits

Our local museum of art organizes an annual fund raiser where local interior decorators come together and create a designer showcase home. The home is on display for a period of time to highlight the designers' work and is then raffled off to raise money for the museum.

Last year I installed full spectrum light bulbs in the ceiling fixtures in the kitchen. When the other designers saw the way the natural light intensified all of the colors and created a "cleaner," more pleasant feel in the kitchen, I had numerous requests for other rooms.

My wife and I especially like the full spectrum bulbs and tubes in the kitchen, bathrooms, fixtures that illuminate art pieces and, of course, in reading lamps.

RECOMMENDATIONS:

- ♦ **Spend as much time as possible outdoors in natural sunlight.**

- ♦ **Utilize full spectrum light bulbs and tubes wherever possible.**
  My preferred brand is *Verilux*, both for clarity of light and long life.

- **Invest in a special natural light "box" that provides 10,000 lux of light when you sit in front of it.** This product is excellent for use when reading, writing letters, paying bills, etc. Some health insurers will pay at least part of the cost when prescribed by a doctor. 30 minutes a day, first thing in the morning, is recommended.

RECOMMENDED PRODUCTS:

- *Living Sunshine* is a table top light box that works to replace the natural benefits of spending a day in the sun without the risks of damaging rays that your skin doesn't need.

- *Verilux* full spectrum bulbs and tubes are available for almost every application. By providing the wider spectrum of light, colors are more vibrant and people notice the difference immediately.

The products listed above are all available from the Home Environment Center.
To order, call 1-888-612-5798
or visit www.YourHealthyHome.com.

ADDITIONAL INFORMATION:
Surviving the Toxic Crisis Dr. William R. Kellas
(ISBN 0 -9636491-1-6)

Light Years Ahead Celestial Arts
(ISBN 0-89087-762-9)

– 13 –
Cosmetics and Personal Care Products

Your body's largest organ is your skin. To understand your skin's ability to absorb chemicals you have only to ask someone who has worn a nicotine patch to quit smoking about the first time they applied the patch. They tasted the chemical in their mouth almost immediately.

For the purpose of our discussion of cosmetics I'd like you to think of everything you apply to your hair and skin: Soaps, shampoos, skin cream, perfumes, makeup, hair spray, nail polish, deodorants, shaving cream, lip protectant, sun screen, etc., etc., *etc.*

The *Journal of the American Medical Association* estimates that $30 billion dollars per year is spent on shampoos, lotions and personal care products.

The *National Institute of Occupational Safety and Health* (NIOSH) has identified nearly 900 toxic chemicals in personal care products. Over 700 of them can cause acute toxic effects. Over 300 of them can cause developmental abnormalities and eye, hair and skin damage.

Dr. Doris Rapp has done extensive research on these issues and believes these chemicals have likely had something to do with the:

- 40% increase in childhood brain cancer in the last 25 years.

- Doubling of testicular cancer cases in just 5 years

- Increase in male pattern baldness in women

- An increase in certain cancers, babies with birth defects and miscarriages among hairdressers

- Increase in sterility in young men

- Increase in allergy and asthma

Some of the more common chemicals causing concern include:

Sodium LAUREL Sulfate

Isopropyl Alcohol

Propylene Glycol

Cocomide DEA / NEA

Methylene Chloride

Paraben

Formaldehyde

Quaternium 15

Diazolidinyl

Diethanolamine (DEA)

Triethanolamine (TEA)

Bronopol

Ethylene dichloride

Here again, not everyone agrees on the level of risk when using products containing these chemicals. I prefer to play it safe and avoid them whenever possible. Please remember, just because the label says "ALL NATURAL INGREDIENTS" doesn't mean the product is free of dangerous chemicals.

Baby Powder

Knowing what we do about inhaled particles, does it make any sense to "dust" our infants with powder? If you use powder, please, do so carefully and limit the amount floating in the air.

Sharing Your Scents With Others

Chemically sensitive people are now found in sufficient numbers that some communities have banned the wearing of perfumes and colognes in public places.

Have you ever picked up a telephone handset that was recently handled by someone wearing a strong perfume or sat near someone in church or at a performance that was heavily "scented?" Many susceptible individuals have no choice but to use a different phone or move to another seat or leave the area altogether. Their throat tightens, nasal passages constrict, heart rate increases and each breath is a struggle. Of course, *it's all in their head,* according to many so-called experts.

Bottom Line: The chemicals in scented products are contributing to our overall "TOXIC LOAD." Each and every exposure is another straw on the camel's back known as your immune system. As the awareness of this issue grows, and more people become susceptible, I believe wearers of perfume and cologne will eventually be viewed by health-minded people much like smokers are today.

RECOMMENDATIONS:
♦ Use as few scented products as possible.
♦ Choose more healthful cosmetics, personal care and hair products over the more toxic products.

**Many healthy personal care products are available from the Home Environment Center.
To order, call 1-888-612-5798
or visit www.YourHealthyHome.com.**

ADDITIONAL INFORMATION:
Don't Go To The Cosmetics Counter Without Me Paula Begoun
(ISBN 1-877-98828-6)

– 14 –
Automobiles

While watching a morning news program I heard the question *"Where is the air quality worse, on a commercial airliner or in our own car?"* The surprising answer given was **"IN YOUR OWN CAR."**

Your car's air conditioning and heating system will condense moisture and grow mold in the system. Most of us park the car all day and, at least during part of the year, the inside temperature is often well over 100 degrees. In the dark, moist, hot conditions in the car's HVAC system, mold grows at an alarming rate. After work, most of us get in the car, start the engine and turn the A/C or heat on high fan . . . and blow all of this mold right in our face! There is also a very real possibility that a number of nasty bacteria inhabit the system as well.

As if the biological "stuff" wasn't enough, let's add some *chemicals* to the mix. That "new car smell" that some people love is really an interesting cocktail of chemical gasses. Plastics, vinyls, foam, fabrics, rubber mats, adhesives and weather stripping all add their outgassing chemicals to the mix of pollutants inside a car. Scented air fresheners and cleaning products also pollute the air in your car with chemicals.

Let's also look at what comes in from outside: exhaust gasses and particulate, rubber dust from tires (already implicated as causing an increased rate of heart disease), as well as naturally occurring pollen and molds.

Exhaust Leaks

One of the most dangerous exposures in the car is your own exhaust if you have a leak in the system. Many deaths and injuries have resulted from inhalation of carbon monoxide (CO) gas inside cars with leaking exhaust systems. Occupants of campers and RVs are at even greater risk if they sleep in their vehicles.

There is obviously only one thing to do with an exhaust leak and that is, of course, to fix it <u>immediately</u>.

Gasoline Odors

If you smell gasoline in or around your vehicle please consider that a critical situation as well. You may have a vapor recovery system leak or, worse yet, a fuel leak. Either way you have a <u>very dangerous situation</u> and need to correct the problem <u>immediately</u>.

Air Purification for Your Car

Not to be confused with an "air freshener" hanging from the rear view mirror!

Air quality in cars is important enough to consumers that most luxury car manufacturers are now equipping their new cars with filtration systems. If your car is so equipped, be sure to service the filters as recommended by the manufacturer. Properly serviced, these filters will reduce particulate transfer into the car through the air conditioner intake. However, they have little if any effect on pollutants off-gassing <u>inside</u> your car or the gasses and odors (diesel exhaust, for example) brought in from outside or created by a smoker or pets <u>inside</u> the vehicle.

Portable, filterless air purifiers are also available. They plug into the cigarette lighter, reduce odors and provide cleaner air in cars, trucks and motor homes.

> *CASE STORY:* The wife of a long distance truck driver I know used to require him to change clothes on the patio before entering the house each time he returned from a driving trip because she couldn't stand the smell of diesel fuel and exhaust on his clothes! He put a small, portable air purifier in his truck and no longer has any odors on his clothes, skin, hair <u>or</u> in the truck. He also tells me he feels less fatigue and is more alert when driving thanks to the fresher, cleaner air in his truck.

RECOMMENDATIONS:

♦ When purchasing a new vehicle, consider models with air filtration systems, preferably with carbon to reduce particulate and chemical infiltration of the interior.

♦ Avoid use of scented products and sprays in your car. They only add more chemicals to your air.

♦ Avoid use of antimicrobial cleaners / sprays in your A/C and heating system. I prefer to circulate ozone through the system to deodorize and sanitize it.

RECOMMENDED PRODUCTS:

♦ The *Living Air Peak* (air purifier) is great for cars, trucks or RV's. For mobile use, plug it into your cigarette lighter. For indoor use a 110v power supply is provided. Great for hotel rooms too!

**This product is available from the
Home Environment Center.
To order, call 1-888-612-5798
or visit www.YourHealthyHome.com.**

SUMMARY

As you can see, we are constantly exposed to environmental influences that are harmful to humans: Some we can "reasonably" control and others we cannot. If we control the exposures we <u>can</u>, we are then better able to handle the ones we cannot.

If we protect our immunity by living in a healthy environment, at some point in the future we will look back and be thankful for the effort we made to protect ourselves from the daily exposure to harmful indoor pollutants. By then far more will be known about the cumulative damage caused by these exposures and those of us who take action <u>today</u> will be much healthier as a result.

To The Allergic and Environmentally Ill

If you are suffering from NON-ignorable allergy-related or environmental illness, DON'T GIVE UP HOPE! Take responsibility for yourself, educate yourself, and don't always expect experts to solve your problem. Reading this book is a great beginning. Now, a thorough inspection of your living environment and a few changes can make a <u>big</u> difference. Most cost little or nothing.

I also suggest you seek out a medical professional who understands environmental illness, preferably one who is a good listener. When the right questions are asked and the answers are heard, useful clues are often uncovered, action can be taken and healing can begin.

To The Families and Friends
of The Allergic and Environmentally Ill

One of the most painful aspects of severe allergies and environmental illness is the disbelief of those closest to us. Many times, even our loved ones, who've never been sick, can't understand the numerous, undiagnosable symptoms and the devastating effect they have on us.

Virtually everyone who lives and/or works indoors is negatively impacted by indoor pollutants and many who are not yet environmentally ill will be in the future. I pray you never have to personally experience this illness to *any* degree to believe in its existence and that you will take steps NOW to improve your own environment.

To Medical Practitioners

In spite of my frustrations with the medical profession, I prefer to believe that doctors all have their patients' best interests at heart. I understand the challenge chronically ill patients who show little or no improvement represent in your practice. I also understand the difficulty you are faced with as the emotional aspect of their illness intensifies. I believe some of these patients leave your office and go home to the very conditions that caused their illness in the first place.

How many times has one of your patients reported feeling better when they go out of town? Did you respond by saying they were under less stress while they were away?

Perhaps this book will cause you to consider the possibility that these patients' symptoms *may* be environmentally induced. Just because the arsenal of tests available to you provides no diagnosis or explanation for their illness, it isn't necessarily "all in their head."

It may be in their HOME.

— APPENDIX —

HEALTHY HOME QUESTIONNAIRE

If you believe someone in your family is experiencing health problems caused by your home, the following questions and checklist may lead you to the cause.

Surprisingly, I often find <u>all</u> of these conditions in the same home.

1) Have you done any painting, carpeting or remodeling?	❑ Yes ❑ No
2) Do you use any scented products in the house, i.e. air fresheners, potpourri, andles, incense, sprays or fabric softeners?	❑ Yes ❑ No
3) Have you had any roof or plumbing leaks in the house? If yes, check the affected area(s) for mold.	❑ Yes ❑ No
4) Have you changed any cleaning products recently? — including laundry products, furniture polish, laundry products, soaps or shampoos?	❑ Yes ❑ No
5) Do you have any gas-fired appliances? If so, do you have a carbon monoxide detector and have you checked for gas leaks?	❑ Yes ❑ No
6) Have your air ducts been inspected and/or cleaned?	❑ Yes ❑ No
7) Have you had your drinking water tested lately? If not, a bacteria test would be a good idea, especially if you're on a private well.	❑ Yes ❑ No
8) Do you have any new pets or pet care products in your home?	❑ Yes ❑ No
9) Do you have any pest infestation problems? — Bats, bees, birds, insects, rodents, etc.?	❑ Yes ❑ No
10) Do you have any pest control chemicals, including moth balls, in the house?	❑ Yes ❑ No
11) Have you added any new furniture or cabinets lately?	❑ Yes ❑ No
12) Do you do any arts and crafts work using paints, inks or glues in the house?	❑ Yes ❑ No
13) If you live in a multi-occupancy building, are your neighbors creating or emitting pollutants and/or odors?	❑ Yes ❑ No

HEALTHY HOME CHECKLIST

For each room in your home, place a ✔ on the appropiate line when you find the condition(s) or need for maintenance as listed below, then take action to correct the situation (continued on page 92).

	MASTER BEDROOM	MASTER BATH	BEDROOM #2	BEDROOM #3	BEDROOM #4	BATH #2	BATH #3	LAUNDRY	BASEMENT	ATTIC	KITCHEN	DEN / LIBRARY	LIVING ROOM	FAMILY ROOM	HALL	FOYER	HEATER CLOSET
Ceiling – Leaks, Stains, Moisture, Mold, Peeling Texture																	
Walls – Moisture, Mold, Peeling Paint																	
Baseboard – Moisture, Mold, Insects, Peeling Paint																	
Windows – Leaks, Latches																	
Cabinets – Leaks, Cleaning Products, Cloths																	
A/C Heater Ducts – Mold, Dirt, Moisture																	
Cold Air Returns – Filter Condition, Mold, Moisture																	
Fireplace – Chimney, Flue Condition, Fire Screen																	
Wood Stove – Chimney, Flue Condition, Fire Screen																	
Oven / Stove – Gas Leak																	
Refer – Interior Mold, Condensation Pan Mold, Dusty Coils, Water Filter																	

HEALTHY HOME CHECKLIST (CON'T)

For each room in your home, place a ✔ on the appropriate line when you find the condition(s) or need for maintenance as listed below, then take action to correct the situation.

	MASTER BEDROOM	MASTER BATH	BEDROOM #2	BEDROOM #3	BEDROOM #4	BATH #2	BATH #3	LAUNDRY	BASEMENT	ATTIC	KITCHEN	DEN / LIBRARY	LIVING ROOM	FAMILY ROOM	HALL	FOYER	HEATER CLOSET
Shower – Chlorine Filter, Leaks, Mold																	
Water Softener – Leaks, Odor, Test Water for Hardness & Bacteria																	
Water Purifier / RO – Last Filter Change & Sanitizing, Leaks, Test Water for Effectiveness (chlorine, total dissolved solids, bacteria)																	
Water Heater – Age, Gas or Water Leaks																	
Washing Machine – Leaks, Age of Hoses																	
Clothes Dryer – Vent Hose Lint, Gas Leak																	
Fire Extinguisher – Check for Last Service																	
CO Detector – Inspect, Install																	

I Need Your Help

While the public awareness of these issues is growing, unfortunately most people don't yet realize the importance of living in a healthy home and <u>too many people are still getting sick</u>.

Each time a newborn baby comes home from the hospital to live in a house full of mold and chemicals another new life starts down the road to chronic illness.

When I see a child using an inhaler to be able to breathe I always wonder about their home and school, what they're breathing and what they've been exposed to.

When I meet someone fighting cancer I ask myself, would their chances for recovery be better if they weren't living in an unhealthy home environment? The answer, of course, is <u>YES</u>!

Please share what you have read here with your family and friends, your doctors and anyone else who will listen. Very few experiences in life are as gratifying as providing someone a key that opens the door to a healthier life. If, after reading this book, you or someone you know has a story you'd like to share with us, please send it to us at info@yourhealthyhome.com.

Right Livelihood

I've had a number of different careers in my life and, with each new beginning, I thought I had found my "right livelihood." In the years following my poisoning as I was regaining my strength and energy I met numbers of people searching for information and products to create healthier homes for their families.

I believe everything happens for a reason and I soon realized I had found my final and most important career. My wife, Michele, and I have spent four years developing the *Home Environment Center* in Tucson and are expanding nationwide. Our goal is to develop a team of part-time and full-time independent representatives working from offices in their homes to serve communities in every state across the country. If you have a sincere interest in these issues and an entrepreneurial spirit, we'd love to hear from you. To learn more about this exciting, timely program, including our training and ongoing support, call us at 1-888-612-5798 or email us at info@yourhealthyhome.com.